Compound Effect

How Small Wins Lead to Big Money Goals

Andrew Galowey

Copyright © [Andrew Galowey] [2024]. All rights reserved. No part of this publication may be reproduced, distributed, or transmitted in any form or by any means, including photocopying, recording, or other electronic or mechanical methods, without the prior written permission of the publisher, except in the case of brief quotations embodied in critical reviews and certain other noncommercial uses permitted by copyright law.

Table Of Contents

Introduction

Chapter 1: Unlocking the Power of Small Wins

Chapter 2: Building the Foundation: Defining Your Financial Goals

Chapter 3: Habit Hacks: Mastering The Daily Grind

Chapter 4: Momentum Builders: Small Wins in Action

Chapter 5: Taming the Dragons: Overcoming Obstacles

Conclusion

Introduction

Have you ever pondered how a little acorn grows into a tall oak? The solution lies in a tremendous force known as the compound effect. Just like a tree becomes stronger with each season, so can your riches. In "The Compound Effect: How Small Wins Lead to Big Money Goals," we'll on a trip to discover the secrets of financial success. We'll look at how apparently tiny behaviors, when repeated repeatedly, may lead to the realization of seemingly unachievable financial objectives. Forget the get-rich-quick scams. This book provides a step-by-step guide to achieving long-term financial stability. We'll provide you the skills and tactics you need to turn your big aspirations into concrete actions, develop healthy money habits, and conquer the inevitable barriers on your journey to financial independence. Are you prepared to see your money snowball? Let us begin!

Chapter 1: Unlocking the Power of Small Wins

Imagine putting a penny in a piggy bank. Not exactly life-changing, right? Imagine yourself contributing a single cent every day for a year. Suddenly, the relatively tiny sum has grown into $3.65. This is the core of the compound effect: a concept with the potential to transform your financial destiny.

Financial success does not mean winning the lottery or inheriting a fortune. It's about leveraging the power of little, consistent acts that add up over time. Your money may bloom from apparently minor everyday actions, just as an acorn grows softly into a towering oak. However, the path to riches paved with pennies takes awareness, dedication, and a mindset change.

Let's face it: the draw of quick satisfaction is great. We desire fast fixes and instant success stories. However, generating long-term wealth is a marathon rather than a sprint. Consider the lotto winner who squanders their winnings overnight. True financial stability is achieved by laying a strong financial foundation one brick at a time.

Here is when the compound effect comes in. It's the alchemy that turns apparently insignificant everyday decisions into a tremendous force moving you toward your financial objectives. Imagine rolling a snowball downward. At first, it is compact and simple to use. But with each rotation, it acquires more snow, increasing its size and momentum. This snowball symbolizes your wealth, and the little, consistent acts - your daily savings deposits, wise financial choices, and healthy money habits - are the snow that drives its development.

However, there are two options in this circumstance. One option is to stand by and watch someone else roll their snowball into a financial castle. Alternatively, you may take a handful of snow (your daily activities) and begin rolling. It may seem little at first, but with each passing day, your snowball gains velocity, becoming bigger and more powerful.

The beauty of the compound effect stems from its inherent simplicity. You don't need a cash windfall to get started. All you need is the commitment to make tiny, persistent adjustments. Consider a common example: your everyday coffee run. Instead of spending $5 on a latte, try making your own coffee. This apparently tiny modification saves you $5 every day. Now increase that by 250 working days each year, and you've saved $1250! Invest that money carefully, and the power of compound interest will grow it into a substantial amount.

This is only one example; the possibilities are unlimited. You may prepare more meals at home instead of dining out, avoid wasteful impulsive purchases, or set aside a small amount of your paycheck to be routinely put into a savings account. These may seem to be little drops in the financial ocean, but keep in mind that the steady drizzle is what fills the bucket.

However, the compound impact is a two-edged sword. Just as modest, regular good acts snowball into riches, negative financial habits may compound, leading you down a road of financial hardship. Skipping gym memberships and eating unhealthy fast food every day may save you money in the short run, but the long-term health effects might cost you dearly. Impulse purchases and wasteful spending may seem innocuous at first, but they may quickly deplete your financial resources.

So, how can we harness the strength of the compound effect to our advantage? Here are some practical measures to help you get started.

- Identify Your Big Money Goals: What does financial freedom mean for you? Do you want to retire early, live debt-free, or achieve financial independence? Defining your long-term objectives is critical for maintaining motivation and making modest, consistent actions.

- Break it Down: Break down your large ambitions into smaller, more doable benchmarks. This will make the road less frightening and give you a feeling of success as you reach each milestone.

Celebrate your progress, no matter how tiny. Recognize that every saved dollar or avoided impulsive buy is a step closer to your final objective.

- Track Your Progress: Having a clear image of your progress, whether via a budgeting tool or a basic notepad, keeps you motivated and accountable.

- Automate When Possible: Creating automated transfers from your checking account to your savings or investment accounts promotes consistency and eliminates the desire to spend.

Remember that compound effect is a long-term game. There will be days when you feel disheartened, and progress may seem sluggish. However, by being dedicated to tiny, persistent activities, you will see the cumulative impact shift your financial picture.

The path to financial independence starts with a single step. Will you take it today?

Chapter 2: Building the Foundation: Defining Your Financial Goals

Any successful financial journey is built on a solid foundation of properly stated money objectives. Even the most dedicated traveler will be lost without a map. In this chapter, we'll go over the critical process of setting your financial goals and turning them into practical activities.

Imagine embarking on a cross-country road journey without a destination. Sure, you may come across some amazing sites along the route, but achieving a specified objective becomes a question of luck. The same logic applies to your financial situation. The value of creating specific money objectives stems from their capacity to bring direction and purpose to your financial actions. They become the guiding light that directs you toward financial stability and enables you to make sound decisions with your hard-earned money.

So, how can you identify your financial goals and turn them into concrete plans? Here's a plan to get you started:

1. Dream Big, Plan Smart: Allow yourself to visualize the life you want. Do you want to retire early, explore the globe, or achieve financial independence? Don't be scared to dream big; these lofty goals will keep you motivated in the long term. However, remember to balance your aspirations with a dose of reality. Break down your long-term ambitions into smaller, more doable ones.

What are some long-term financial goals?

- Early Retirement: Determine the age you want to retire and the yearly income required to maintain your preferred lifestyle.
- Debt-Free Living: Identify all of your debts (credit cards, school loans, etc.) and devise a repayment strategy,

focusing on high-interest obligations first.
- Financial Independence: Determine how much passive income you'll need to pay your living expenditures, enabling you to work by choice rather than need.

2. Embrace the Power of Numbers: Once you have a clear vision of your long-term goals, measure them. This entails putting a monetary value to your objectives and determining the timeframe for completion. While unanticipated events may demand changes, having a ballpark number gives you a sense of direction and helps you to design a tailored approach.

Let's use an example:

- Goal: Early retirement at age 50, with an annual income of $75,000.

Calculate how much you need to save and invest to create $75,000 in passive income each year. This will include characteristics such as your present age, risk tolerance, and predicted investment returns. Financial planning tools and internet calculators might be useful throughout this process.

3. Prioritization is essential: Life is filled with conflicting wants, and your money are no different. You may covet a lavish trip while yet seeking financial stability. This is where priority comes in. Determine your most essential financial objectives and invest money appropriately.

Here are some questions to help you prioritize:

- Urgency: What objectives deserve urgent attention? Are there any immediate bills or short-term demands that must be handled first?
- influence: Which objectives will have the most influence on your overall financial health?

- Alignment with Values: Are your financial objectives consistent with your underlying values? For example, if environmental sustainability is essential to you, you may prioritize investing in environmentally friendly businesses.

4. Embrace the Art of Delayed satisfaction: The road to financial success is paved with wise decisions, not quick satisfaction. There may be occasions when you feel tempted to buy that fancy purse or the newest device. This is where delayed gratification comes in. Developing the discipline to put long-term objectives ahead of short-term demands is critical for financial success.

Here are some ways for embracing delayed gratification.

- The 24-Hour Rule: Set a waiting time before making impulsive purchases. Often, the initial thrill subsides,

enabling you to make a more informed choice.
- Reward Yourself Strategically: Celebrate financial successes with non-monetary incentives. For example, reward yourself with a peaceful day at the park after meeting a financial goal.

5. The Power of "What If?": Financial planning is a dynamic process. Life throws curveballs, and your objectives may need to change along the road. Create a practice of asking oneself "what if?" situations. What happens if you lose your job? What if your medical expenditures increase? Prepare for unexpected events by setting up an emergency fund and developing a backup plan.

Defining your money objectives is the first critical step toward financial independence. Following these stages will turn your aspirations into actionable strategies, allowing you to make educated financial decisions and attain long-term financial stability. Remember, the path ahead may appear.

Chapter 3: Habit Hacks: Mastering The Daily Grind

Financial success does not happen immediately. It's a marathon, not a sprint, driven by regular everyday practices. Consider yourself an athlete practicing for a race. Just as regular exercise improves strength and endurance, good money habits improve financial health. In this chapter, we'll look at techniques for developing strong financial habits and conquering the daily grind.

Let's face it: our natural tendencies often drive us toward rapid satisfaction. We desire short fixes, impulsive purchases that provide a transient sensation of fulfillment. However, financial success is built on regular, beneficial behaviors that compound over time. What is the good news? Cultivating these behaviors is simpler than you may believe. Here are some practical measures to help you get started.

1. Identify Your Money Kryptonite: Everyone has money vulnerabilities. Perhaps it's internet shopping sprees, costly restaurant dinners, or spontaneous purchases at the checkout. Identifying your particular "money kryptonite" is the first step in developing a defensive plan.

Here are several techniques to identify your spending weaknesses:

- Track your expenses: Using budgeting applications or a basic notepad, record your everyday expenditures for a month. This will highlight trends and locations where your money might be falling through the gaps.
- Be honest with yourself: Recognize your spending triggers. Is it boredom that prompts internet purchasing sprees? Perhaps social pressure forces you to continue with pricey excursions. Understanding the

emotions that drive your spending is essential to modifying your habit.

2. Replacing Bad behaviors with Good Ones: Now that you've discovered your financial shortcomings, it's important to replace them with good behaviors. Don't attempt to completely revamp your financial situation overnight. Begin small, focusing on replacing one poor behavior with a positive one. Here are few examples:

- Swap the latte habit: Instead of going out for a $5 coffee every day, prepare your own. The savings accumulate dramatically over time.
- Unsubscribe from temptation: Unsubscribe from marketing communications that lead to impulsive purchases. Out of sight and out of memory!
- Accept the "No Spend Weekend" challenge: Set yourself the goal of spending no money on useless

purchases during the weekend. It's a fun approach to reduce impulsive purchases and become more conscious of your spending.

3. The Power of Automation: Human willpower is fickle. We all have times of weakness. Fortunately, technology can come to our rescue. Automating your money reduces dependence on willpower while ensuring constant growth. Here are a few methods to use automation:

- Create automatic transfers from your checking account to your savings or investment accounts. The "pay yourself first" technique assures constant savings.
- Automate bill payments: Set up automated bill payments to prevent late penalties and keep your finances organized.
- Consider a robo-advisor if you want to invest without having to do anything.

These automated systems will manage your assets depending on your risk tolerance and financial objectives.

4. Embrace the Buddy System: Financial planning does not have to be a solo endeavor. Partnering with a friend or family member who has similar financial objectives may be an effective motivation. Here are some methods to harness the potential of a financial buddy system:

- Maintain accountability by regularly discussing your financial successes and issues with your spouse. Having someone to celebrate accomplishments and sympathize on disappointments may be quite motivating.
- Share resources and strategies: Share financial advice and resources to assist each other remain on track with your financial objectives.

- Create a "no-judgment zone" by approaching your interactions with empathy and support. Financial paths are unique, and open communication creates a comfortable environment for expressing problems.

5. The Power of Positive Reinforcement: Developing new behaviors requires time and effort. Celebrate your progress, no matter how tiny. Rewarding yourself for reaching financial goals encourages good behavior and keeps you motivated. However, choose non-monetary prizes. For example, after meeting your savings goal, reward yourself with a peaceful day at the spa.

Remember, developing good financial habits is a marathon, not a sprint. There will be setbacks and days when temptation prevails. Do not beat yourself up; instead, take it as a learning experience and get back on track. Consistency is essential. By adopting these habit hacks into your daily routine, you'll be well on your way to conquering the daily grind and setting yourself up for financial success. Small, consistent measures taken now will snowball into a secure financial future. So, lace up your financial running shoes and prepare for an amazing adventure ahead!

Chapter 4: Momentum Builders: Small Wins in Action

The path to financial independence is paved with tiny victories. These apparently little efforts, when repeated on a regular basis, add up over time, driving you closer to your financial objectives. Imagine yourself ascending a mountain. Every step, no matter how tiny, moves you closer to the top. In this chapter, we'll look at practical ways for adopting tiny victories in a variety of financial areas, converting your daily routine into a wealth-generating engine.

Savings Strategies:

- Embrace the Power of Change: Round up your everyday expenditures to the closest dollar and put the difference in a savings account. This "round-up" approach uses the power of modest contributions to accumulate a large savings pool over time.

The 52-Week Challenge is a fun savings challenge in which you put away a specified amount each week depending on the week number. You begin with $1 in week one, $2 in week two, and so on, eventually reaching $52 in the final week. By the end of the year, you'll have earned a cool $1,378!

Use the "No Spend Days" challenge to commit to no needless spending on certain days. This may be a weekly or monthly activity that forces you to be more conscious of your everyday expenditures while also exposing areas where you can cut down.

Debt repayment strategies:

The Snowball Method is a debt repayment approach that emphasizes paying off the lowest debt first, regardless of interest rates. Quick successes create a feeling of achievement and boost desire to tackle bigger obligations.

The Avalanche Method focuses on repaying loans with the highest interest rates first. While it may not provide the same psychological lift as the snowball approach, it may save you money in the long term by reducing interest payments.

The Debt Consolidation Shuffle involves combining high-interest loans into a single loan with a reduced interest rate. This streamlines the repayment process and saves you money on interest rates, freeing up resources for speedier debt removal.

Investment Strategies:

Embrace Micro-Investing: Platforms such as robo-advisors enable you to invest modest sums on a regular basis, making them ideal for novices or those on a restricted budget. Even a few dollars invested regularly may reap the benefits of compound interest over time.

Invest Your Spare Change: Use applications to round up your everyday purchases and invest the difference in fractional stocks or ETFs. This simple method enables you to put your spare change to work for your long-term financial objectives.

- The Max Out Strategy: If your business provides a 401(k) with matching contributions, prioritize increasing your contribution to take advantage of the free money your employer contributes to your retirement. It's a definite victory!

Budget Hacks:

- The 50/30/20 Rule: Divide your income into three categories: 50% for necessities (rent, electricity, food), 30% for desires (entertainment, eating out), and 20% for savings and debt reduction. This basic approach promotes smart spending and prioritizes your financial objectives.

- Embrace the Cash Envelope System: Each week, withdraw a certain amount of cash for discretionary spending and divide it into categories (groceries, eating out, etc.). Once the money is gone, the expenditure stops, encouraging responsible planning and avoiding excess.

- Utilize Budgeting tools: Use free or low-cost budgeting tools to monitor your income and expenditures, classify your spending, and find areas for improvement.

Remember that consistency is crucial. The force of the action is not in its enormity, but in its consistency over time. Celebrate your minor victories, no matter how insignificant they may seem. Each dollar saved, each debt payment made, and each sensible investment choice brings you closer to meeting your financial objectives.

By adding these momentum generators into your everyday routine, you can turn apparently trivial activities into a tremendous force that propels you toward financial independence. The snowball of riches begins with a single determined deed. Are you ready to take yours up and go rolling?

Chapter 5: Taming the Dragons: Overcoming Obstacles

Financial independence is not always easy to achieve. There will be difficulties and barriers along the route, as well as hidden dragons ready to disrupt your progress. These dragons may take various forms, including emotional outbursts, procrastination, peer pressure, and even unexpected life occurrences. In this chapter, we'll provide you the skills and techniques you need to defeat these financial monsters while remaining dedicated to your quest.

Dragon of Emotional Spending:

Emotional spending is many people's worst nightmare. Whether it's retail therapy to relieve stress or spontaneous purchases motivated by boredom, emotional spending may derail your financial objectives. Here's how to tame the dragon:

- Identify Your Triggers: The first step is to identify what emotions cause your buying sprees. Is it melancholy, loneliness, or anxiety? Once you've identified your emotional triggers, you may work on healthy coping techniques.

- Create Alternative Outlets: Discover healthy methods to express your feelings. Take a stroll in nature, spend time with loved ones, or explore a creative interest.

- Accept the Waiting Period: Follow the "24-hour rule." Wait 24 hours before making an impulsive buy. Often, the initial impulse passes, allowing for a more reasoned conclusion.

The Dragon of Procrastination:

Procrastination is another prevalent financial enemy. Delaying chores such as budgeting, setting up automated transfers, and investigating investment possibilities might slow your financial progress. Here's how to defeat the dragon:

- Break Down Big Tasks: Being intimidated by a seemingly difficult activity, such as making a budget, is a recipe for procrastination. Divide huge activities into smaller, more doable segments.

- Schedule Time for Action: Set aside particular periods in your schedule for financial planning. Treat these visits as crucial meetings, and prevent distractions.

- Reward Yourself for Progress: Recognize your achievements, no matter how minor. Completing a budget or exploring investment opportunities warrants a prize!

Dragon of Peer Pressure:

Trying to keep up with the Joneses may be a major financial burden. Friends or family members who live expensive lives may entice you to splurge in order to maintain a particular impression. Here's how you can defend yourself.

- Define Your Values: Concentrate on what is actually important to you, not what others value. Financial stability and peace of mind are much more important than following transient trends.

- Communicate Your aspirations: Tell your friends and family about your financial aspirations. True friends would encourage you to pursue your goals rather than pressuring you to depart from them.

- Concentrate on Your Journey: Do not compare your financial chapter to someone else's full book. Everyone's financial path is unique; concentrate on your development and appreciate your achievements.

Dragon of Unexpected Events:

Life throws curveballs. Job loss, medical issues, or unforeseen repairs may all disrupt your financial goals. Here's how to prepare for these unexpected dragons.

- Build an Emergency Fund: Set aside 3-6 months' worth of living costs in an emergency fund to weather unanticipated financial storms.

- Review Your Insurance Coverage: Make sure you have enough health, auto, and renters/homeowners insurance to protect yourself from financial ruin in the event of an accident or emergency.

- Maintain Financial Flexibility: Be aware of your fixed and variable costs. Look for places where you may reduce down to ensure financial security during difficult times.

Remember that overcoming hurdles is an important component of reaching your financial objectives. Don't let disappointments discourage you. Learn from them, make adjustments to your strategy as needed, and remain dedicated to your path. Financial difficulties are only temporary; however, your dedication to your financial well-being is everlasting.

By arming yourself with the necessary skills and methods, you can defeat these financial dragons and emerge stronger on the other side. Remember that financial independence requires persistence and perseverance. Accept the hurdles, appreciate your triumphs, and keep working towards your financial goals.

Conclusion

The path to financial independence is not a sprint to the finish line, but rather a marathon of steady, deliberate steps. You've now got the skills and techniques you need to unleash the power of the compound effect and develop long-term wealth by capitalizing on little successes. Remember that it is not about instant miracles; it is about committing to everyday development, prioritizing your objectives, and overcoming barriers.

As you begin on this exciting path, remember the value of constant action. Every dollar saved, every good financial choice made, and every step ahead builds a solid foundation for your financial future. Allow this book to be your constant companion, a reminder that the secret to financial success is not in spectacular gestures, but in the everyday decisions you make.

So, are you prepared to see your riches snowball? Take a deep breath, commit to action, and watch your financial ambitions become a reality. The ability to attain financial independence is within you. Go out, conquer!

www.ingramcontent.com/pod-product-compliance
Lightning Source LLC
Chambersburg PA
CBHW071221240526
45470CB00018B/2194